IOANNIS VASILEIOU

ENTERPRISES
IN THE EUROPEAN UNION

MONOPOLIES - CARTELS

STATE AID - COMPETITION RULES

ATHENS 2019

PUBLISHED IN GREEK BY HISTORICAL QUEST IN 2018

TRANSLATED INTO ENGLISH IN 2019

TRANSLATED BY THE AUTHOR HIMSELF

ART DIRECTOR: SOFIA LIVIERATOU

ACKNOWLEDGEMENTS
To my beloved Maria Nikou
for her encouragement and moral support

TABLE OF CONTENTS

INTRODUCTION: BOOK STRUCTURE

AND TARGETS .... page 9

CHAPTER 1: CONCEPT AND SIGNIFICANCE OF

EUROPEAN UNION COMPETITION

RULES: HOW ARE ENTERPRISES

PRECISELY AFFECTED? .... page 17

CHAPTER 2: EUROPEAN UNION INSTITUTIONS

IN THE CONTEXT OF COMPETITION

RULES .... page 42

CHAPTER 3: CONCLUDING REMARKS .... page 61

BIBLIOGRAPHY .... page 67

INTRODUCTION

BOOK STRUCTURE AND TARGETS

The design and implementation of rational competition rules has always been a top priority of the European Union (EU). Over the years, this priority has become a necessity. The global economic and financial crisis has resulted in numerous economic and social problems the EU is still trying to resolve (European Commission, 2016; European Commission, 2017; European Union/Competition, 2017; Pelagidis and Mitsopoulos, 2014; Vasileiou, 2013a, 2014a, 2017b and 2017c).

We argue that the much-needed economic recovery is irrefutably feasible, but still a variety of thorny issues seek a radical solution. A certain readjustment in terms of both the planning and execution of specific strategies and policies was absolutely necessary and, hence, the Union has been continuously operating towards that direction (European Commission, 2016; European Commission, 2017; European Union/Competition, 2017; Pelagidis and Mitsopoulos, 2014; Vasileiou, 2013a, 2014a, 2017b and 2017c).

In this context, the overriding pursuit is still the respect and strict following of fairer rules for enterprises. The Union objectives for the time being are extremely difficult. Incontrovertibly, their realization will provide us with a clearer picture of what its citizens should expect in the near and distant future.

Fair competition among companies has always been a critical factor for growth, prosperity and innovation. The dominant targets are a) price reductions, b) quality enhancement, c) efficiency maximization, d) a further entrepreneurship encouragement and e) an increase in terms of the range of consumer choice (Europa, 2017; European Commission, 2016; European Commission, 2017; European Commission/Jobs, 2016; European Union/Competition, 2017; Vasileiou, 2013a, 2014a, 2017b and 2017c).

The Union has so far been engaged in intensified efforts not only to effectively protect small businesses, but also to avoid supporting all kinds of troubled ones. The immediate realization of these goals will indisputably result in multiple benefits.

More specifically, for the period 2015-19, the European Commission focuses on the following 10 key priorities, which practically cover the entire spectrum of its policies: a) jobs, growth and investment b) a more functional internal market, c) an increased emphasis on the climate and the energy union in order to make energy more sustainable, secure and affordable, d) a much more balanced and progressive trade policy characterized by the rational exploitation of globalization, e) a deeper and fairer economic and monetary union, which will have the potential of combining stability with democratic accountability, f) a satisfactory digital single market, g) a European agenda in terms of migration, h) the effective preservation of the rule of law in close combination with an improved and far more fruitful cooperation between different justice systems of the Union, i) the continuous pursuit of a more democratic Union and j) the Union's transformation into a much stronger global actor (Alexiou, 2001; Bambra and Eikemo, 2009; Bartolomew et al., 1995; Blanchflower and Shadforth, 2009; Brine, 2002; Calmfors, 2001; Christodoulakis and Mamatzakis, 2009; Coombes and Raybould, 2004; Daveri et al., 2000; Dieckhoff, 2011; Ederveen et al., 2007; European Commission, 2016; European Commission, 2017; European Union/Competition, 2017; Feld, 2005; Fialová and Schneider, 2009; Fragoulis et al., 2004; Gobbin and Van Aarle, 2001; Heinrich and Hildebrand, 2005; Janáčková, 1998; Kazamaki Ottersten, 2004; Kinsella and Kinsella, 2011; Kogan, 2004; Lipsmeyer and Zhu, 2011; Mahler et al., 2000; Newell and Pastore, 2006; Núñez and Livanos, 2010; Öster and Agell, 2007; Overman et al., 2002; Palazuelos-Martinez, 2007; Pelagidis and Mitsopoulos, 2014; Petrongolo and Pissarides, 2008; Pollmann-Schult and Büchel, 2005; Pratschke, 1981; Scott and Kelleher, 1996; Smith, 2011; Stanef, 2012; Stewart, 2005; Sweeney, 1994; Tatsiramos, 2009; Vasileiou, 2013a, 2014a, 2017b and 2017c; Vintrová, 2004; Walsh, 2000; Welbers, 2011; Zamfir, 2011).

As we can easily understand, the issues of competition rules and the proper operation of businesses are included within the context of the majority of the aforementioned priorities and are indisputably vital parameters for economic growth, which is a pivotal factor for social harmony and stability.

The Union's valuable assistance in terms of competition rules will increase optimism for all member states without exception and will contribute towards a better economic future. Nonetheless, in order for this to become a reality, certain conditions must be met without which we might not be able to hope.

In order to proceed to a more coherent categorization, we would argue that, in accordance with Union rules, enterprises are prohibited from a) abusing their dominant position in the context of a particular market with the ultimate aim of excluding weaker competitors, b) fixing prices or even carving up markets among themselves and c) merging in order to be capable of controlling the market (European Commission, 2016; European Union/Competition, 2017; Vasileiou, 2013a, 2014a, 2017b and 2017c).

As far as the merger rule is concerned, regrettably the results are still far from being regarded as positive since only a small number of mergers is being prevented. We strongly believe that such a fact must be of particular concern and it is absolutely essential for a satisfactory solution to be found in favor of the full application of the rule. It is underlined that any mergers between large companies with significant activity in the Union, which take place without prior approval of the European Commission, are expressly prohibited even if these enterprises are based outside the Union (European Union/Competition, 2017; Vasileiou, 2013a, 2014a, 2017b and 2017c).

Numerous prominent scholars, as for example Anton, Antony, Arndt, Berent-Braun, Bönte, Burger, Cordeiro, de Wit, Danciu, Dijkshoorn, Duh, Dunham, Dyker, Frater, Ilbery, Jackson, Jaklič, Jarvis, Jenkins, Jeurissen, Kühne, Kumar, Labib, Lynch-Wood, Major, Mitu, Nielen, Ortiz Avram, Parker, Perrini, Petrakos, Rebernik, Russo, Sarkis, Schmidpeter, Shankar, Spence, Steen Knudsen, Sternberg, Svetličič, Tencati, Tominc, Uhlaner, Vasquez-Brust, von Weltzien Heivik and Williamson, have extensively published in top-class scientific journals on small and medium-sized enterprises (SMEs), which the Union is literally obliged to protect.

Their articles have proved to be of paramount importance and maximum utility in the wider context of our efforts to support the foremost arguments on which this book has been based. Through the (incontrovertibly brilliant) work of the abovementioned authors, we have been given the remarkable opportunity to sufficiently conduct an adequate critical review of SMEs, their momentousness and their specific characteristics.

Furthermore, our dominant aim is to enrich the text with the "critical dimension", avoiding in any way the sterile citation of data. We truly believe that the conclusions drawn are in fact helping the reader to compare them with his own and eventually come up with personal considerations and remarks regarding, for example, whether and to what extent compliance with the already analyzed competition rules affects key issues such as unemployment or the globalization consequences in general

(Alexiou, 2001; Bambra and Eikemo, 2009; Bartolomew et al., 1995; Blanchflower and Shadforth, 2009; Brine, 2002; Calmfors, 2001; Christodoulakis and Mamatzakis, 2009; Coombes and Raybould, 2004; Daveri et al., 2000; Dieckhoff, 2011; Ederveen et al., 2007; European Commission, 2016; European Commission, 2017; European Union/Competition, 2017; Feld, 2005; Fialová and Schneider, 2009; Fragoulis et al., 2004; Gobbin and Van Aarle, 2001; Heinrich and Hildebrand, 2005; Janáčková, 1998; Kazamaki Ottersten, 2004; Kinsella and Kinsella, 2011; Kogan, 2004; Lipsmeyer and Zhu, 2011; Mahler et al., 2000; Newell and Pastore, 2006; Núñez and Livanos, 2010; Öster and Agell, 2007; Overman et al., 2002; Palazuelos-Martinez, 2007; Pelagidis and Mitsopoulos, 2014; Petrongolo and Pissarides, 2008; Pollmann-Schult and Büchel, 2005; Pratschke, 1981; Scott and Kelleher, 1996; Smith, 2011; Stanef, 2012; Stewart, 2005; Sweeney, 1994; Tatsiramos, 2009; Vasileiou, 2013a, 2014a, 2017b and 2017c; Vintrová, 2004; Walsh, 2000; Welbers, 2011; Zamfir, 2011).

Apart from the introduction, the book comprises three more chapters. Chapter 1 is titled *"Concept and Significance of European Union Competition Rules: How are Enterprises Precisely Affected?"*.

In the context of this chapter, there is an attempt to simplify the meaning of the term "competition rules". If we compare this book with the existing literature on these issues, we would claim that this term is used very often, but is not sufficiently clear.

Our aim is the provision of a more complete picture of the term through the use of simple language and comprehensive writing.

Additionally, particular attention must be paid to the fact that in this chapter we attempt to elucidate the precise impact of the Union's competition rules on enterprises. We emphasize that the Union's guiding principle is always the general interest of its citizens and we hope that our scrutiny eventually justifies such a claim.

In Chapter 2, the *"European Union Institutions in the Context of Competition Rules"* are being rigorously presented. These are a) the European Parliament, b) the Council of the EU, c) the European Commission, d) the European Economic and Social Committee, and e) the Committee of the Regions.

Special emphasis is placed on a) the two committees of the Parliament (the Committee on the Internal Market and Consumer Protection and the Committee on Economic and Monetary Affairs), b) the Competitiveness Council, c) the European Economic and Social Committee's Section for the Single Market, Production and Consumption and d) the Commission for Economic Policy of the Committee of the Regions. The abovementioned spectrum is particularly broad and extremely complex, but we hope that the method we have used leads to a functional simplification.

Finally, in Chapter 3, a summary of the foremost points is being presented with the aim of drawing out the main *"Concluding Remarks"*. In simple words, the principal findings are being highlighted, the present level of progress is being examined, the major existing problems are being discussed and the most significant future prospects are being analyzed.

We remain convinced that in both the near and the distant future competition rules will remain an issue of paramount significance. Therefore, it is inevitable that the Union's actions will be constantly scrutinized by entrepreneurs, consumers, politicians and economists. Indubitably, the EU has so far performed gigantic steps towards the coveted economic recovery, and it is undeniable that positive effects have already begun to appear.

CHAPTER 1

CONCEPT AND SIGNIFICANCE OF EUROPEAN UNION COMPETITION RULES: HOW ARE ENTERPRISES PRECISELY AFFECTED?

As we have already mentioned, protecting small businesses and avoid supporting troubled ones, particularly these days, are fundamental EU priorities for a more optimistic tomorrow (Anton et al., 1996; Antony et al., 2008; Bönte and Nielen, 2011; Cordeiro et al., 2012; Duh et al., 2009; Dyker, 2001; Jarvis et al., 2002; Jenkins, 2006; Major, 2008; Ortiz Avram and Kühne, 2008; Parker, 1999; Perrini, 2006; Petrakos, 1996; Russo and Perrini, 2010; Russo and Tencati, 2009; Spence and Schmidpeter, 2003; Steen Knudsen, 2013; Sternberg and Arndt, 2001; Svetličič et al., 2007; Uhlaner et al., 2012; von Weltzien Heivik and Shankar, 2011).

Since the beginning of the global economic and financial crisis, the Union has been continuously characterized by high unemployment rates and low investment levels. The Commission's overriding objective is the reversal of this situation in order for Europe to be able to experience growth pretty soon. The increase of jobs is regarded as indispensable and is directly related to the fair implementation of competition rules. Nonetheless, we stress that this must take place without creating a new debt, which will inevitably lead to a sharp deterioration of the already fragile situation (Alexiou, 2001; Bambra and Eikemo, 2009; Bartolomew et al., 1995; Blanchflower and Shadforth, 2009; Brine, 2002; Calmfors, 2001; Christodoulakis and Mamatzakis, 2009; Coombes and Raybould, 2004; Daveri et al., 2000; Dieckhoff, 2011; Ederveen et al., 2007; Europa, 2017; European Commission, 2016; European Commission/Jobs, 2016; European Union/Competition, 2017; Feld, 2005; Fialová and Schneider, 2009; Fragoulis et al., 2004; Gobbin and Van Aarle, 2001; Heinrich and Hildebrand, 2005; Janáčková, 1998; Kazamaki Ottersten, 2004; Kinsella and Kinsella, 2011; Kogan, 2004; Lipsmeyer and Zhu, 2011; Mahler et al., 2000; Newell and Pastore, 2006; Núñez and Livanos, 2010; Öster and Agell, 2007; Overman et al., 2002; Palazuelos-Martinez, 2007; Pelagidis and Mitsopoulos, 2014; Petrongolo and Pissarides, 2008; Pollmann-Schult and Büchel, 2005; Pratschke, 1981; Scott and Kelleher, 1996; Smith, 2011; Stanef, 2012; Stewart, 2005; Sweeney, 1994; Tatsiramos, 2009; Vasileiou, 2013a, 2014a, 2017b and 2017c; Vintrová, 2004; Walsh, 2000; Welbers, 2011; Zamfir, 2011).

We realize that balance is extremely problematic, so manipulations must be governed by "surgical precision" actions. Any mistakes or omissions cost too much and may lead the Union and its citizens in new, far more unpleasant adventures.

In this chapter, inter alia, vital issues for the coveted economic recovery, such as mergers, state aid, monopolies, and the abuse of dominant position are being critically discussed. We hope that in the end of this chapter, the reader will have fully understood the momentousness of the abovementioned issues and the serious problems that can arise from a misguided addressing or an incomplete organization.

The Union is determined to combat all anticompetitive practices in order for fair competition to be promoted, which obviously serves the general interest and places the Union and its citizens on the path of prosperity, growth and progress.

Ever since the 1950s, European competition policy has been a fundamental component. In particular, in 1957, under the Treaty of Rome, a specific "regime" aiming towards a healthy competition within the common market became a reality (Europa, 2017; European Commission, 2016; European Commission, 2017; European Commission/Jobs, 2016; European Union/Competition, 2017; Vasileiou, 2013a, 2013b, 2014a, 2017b and 2017c).

Through our hitherto conducted research and in the light of EU declarations, positions and strategies, we can incontrovertibly conclude that the protection and proper functioning of SMEs is a crucial factor, particularly from the beginning of the crisis onwards (Anton et al., 1996; Antony et al., 2008; Bönte and Nielen, 2011; Cordeiro et al., 2012; Duh et al., 2009; Dyker, 2001; Jarvis et al., 2002; Jenkins, 2006; Major, 2008; Ortiz

Avram and Kühne, 2008; Parker, 1999; Perrini, 2006; Petrakos, 1996; Russo and Perrini, 2010; Russo and Tencati, 2009; Spence and Schmidpeter, 2003; Steen Knudsen, 2013; Sternberg and Arndt, 2001; Svetličič et al., 2007; Uhlaner et al., 2012; von Weltzien Heivik and Shankar, 2011).

For that reason, it does not seem strange that those specific enterprises have occasionally been rigorously scrutinized by numerous notable scholars worldwide. Hence, we consider that the critical presentation of certain key points that can be discovered in a number of significant studies published in some of the world's most prestigious scientific journals is indeed worth taking place.

We avoid entering into too many specific details, as the book is of a general nature, but we methodically list our major findings in order to provide the reader with impetus and "food for thought" for further study and research.

More specifically, Antony et al. (2008), deal with whether the Six Sigma strategy, which is about business administration, applies to the United Kingdom's manufacturing SMEs. Spence and Schmidpeter (2003) carry out an in-depth research in terms of SMEs' social capital. In particular, they attempt a tremendously interesting critical comparison between firms located in Munich and West London, specializing in a) garages, b) food manufacturing and production, and c) marketing services.

Cordeiro et al. (2012) conduct a critical evaluation of technical efficiency and management correlates in relation to the outstandingly significant issue of solid waste management by Welsh SMEs, while Ortiz Avram and Kühne (2008) refer to implementation issues with regard to responsible business behavior from a "strategic management" perspective, in the context of Austrian SMEs.

Parker (1999) concentrated on the political changes that took place in Europe while authoring her article. These alterations aimed at further supporting SMEs. The conclusion drawn was that those changes indeed benefited SMEs, as they led not only to the proper development of specific programs for their support, but also to deregulatory measures in general, with the functional improvement of the economic environment for business as their predominant pursuit.

What is particularly noteworthy, though, is that Parker expresses a slightly pessimistic view as to whether and to what extent SMEs actually contribute to the burning issues of innovation and employment. She argues that SMEs with a substantial contribution to these issues were actually limited (while her article was being authored), also emphasizing the fact that policies to support SMEs need to be shaped according to SME's diversity.

Parker strongly supports the fact that initiatives and actions aimed at facilitating both the creation and the development of high quality SMEs must rely on specific programs rather than general measures, such as for example tax reduction or labor market deregulation.

These specific programs (expectedly in our opinion) include the systematic support and promotion of research and development, the effective enhancement of the so-called "intangible investments" of the SMEs as well as the tremendously notable regional access to capital and technology. We finally point out that, in the context of her article, Parker systematically focuses on SME-related issues in France, Germany and Sweden.

Perrini (2006) links SMEs to the Theory of Corporate Social Responsibility (CSR Theory) in the case of Italy, while Russo and Perrini (2010) examine the concept of corporate social responsibility in the context of both large firms and SMEs.

Russo and Tencati (2009) also deal with the strategies of corporate social responsibility and via their interesting research they manage to collect significant data regarding not only SMEs but also micro, small, and large firms in Italy. Jenkins (2006), also deals with the issue of corporate social responsibility, but limits her analysis within the United Kingdom.

Jarvis et al. (2002) also focus on the United Kingdom and their analysis refers to the always noteworthy rural industrialization.

In general, they argue that, traditionally, studies on rural industrialization in the United Kingdom have sought to provide an explanation of the success of rural SMEs, in the context of their ability regarding their innovative or enterprising behavior.

This had actually led researchers to concentrate mostly on the material aspects of competitive behavior and more specifically on issues related to technology, at the expense of more intangible aspects such as the advantages of new working practices and marketing strategies in general.

Jarvis et al. refer to the fact that the concept of quality as a pivotal factor of competitive behavior was somewhat neglected in the studies on rural industrialization, despite the fact that at the same time this concept was of increasing appreciation and emphasis in terms of the literature on rural SMEs in the food, farming and craft sectors. The authors meticulously focus on South Warwickshire and North Devon in order to explore the role of quality as a key factor in terms of the competitive advantage.

Sternberg and Arndt (2001) attempt to provide a satisfactory answer regarding which are the decisive factors in terms of the behavior of European firms in general and especially SMEs, as far as innovation is concerned. These two authors conduct a truly remarkable critical presentation accompanied by a thorough examination of two basic hypotheses.

The first refers to the fact that factors related to the firm are more notable compared to those related to the region or other external factors. The second is that in regions characterized by high-level technology and dominated by few but large firms, the behavior of smaller ones with regard to innovation is more affected by regional factors rather than by factors internal to the firm.

According to the authors and following their noteworthy

research, the first hypothesis is indeed verified while the second is not. Taking into account the particular notability of innovation factors at firm level in the European regions examined in the article, the two authors suggest that local innovation policy should be more focused on the exact needs of SMEs in specific areas rather than improving general regional conditions for innovation.

This article, despite the fact that it was published in 2001, remains extremely interesting, since it affects a variety of pivotal issues that appear very often.

Svetličič et al. (2007) focus on the scrupulous examination of differences in terms of outward foreign direct investment actions between large enterprises and SMEs in Poland, Slovenia, Estonia, Czech Republic and Hungary, while Uhlaner et al. (2012) refer to the thorny issue of environmental management practices by the Dutch SMEs. Via their interesting research, they conclude that endogenous factors, such as a) the firm size, b) the sector's tangibility, c) family influence, d) innovative orientation and e) the anticipated financial benefits from the coveted energy conservation can actually contribute to numerous predictions in terms of SMEs commitment level as far as specific environmental management practices are concerned.

Von Weltzien Heivik and Shankar (2011) scrutinize the manner by which SMEs, which are in a cluster, have the potential to successfully respond to global demand in terms of corporate responsibility, while Duh et al. (2009) meticulously concentrate on the issue of the significance of family enterprises in "transition economies".

In general, Duh et al. argue that (based on the data at the time the article was being authored) empirical investigations that had taken place in the "post-socialist" transition economies regarding the importance of family enterprises, were not enough.

The authors use Slovenia as the only case study for empirical examination, but, concurrently, they conduct a particularly useful critical analysis on family enterprises in Croatia, Hungary, Bulgaria and Poland.

In the case of Slovenia, both the structure and the notability of family SMEs in general are being rigorously examined, highlighting the economic significance and the differences in performance and internationalization between family and non-family enterprises.

Dyker (2001) also concentrates on Central and Eastern European economies of accession to the Union, emphasizing the outstandingly important concepts of social capability and technology absorption. Although the article was published in 2001, it remains interesting as numerous people are still dealing with the abovementioned concepts. In the context of his article, Dyker not only refers to SMEs but also provides a wider picture of the situation of these specific economies at that particular time, making noteworthy references to the always critical issue of European integration.

Petrakos (1996) also refers to Central and East European countries, scrutinizing issues related to the development of small enterprises and regional policy. Major (2008) focuses on the case of Hungary and examines the technical efficiency, the allocative efficiency and the profitability of Hungarian SMEs, while Anton et al. (1996) concentrate on the analysis of the SMEs specific role in the context of regional redevelopment in Romania.

Steen Knudsen (2013) carefully investigates the tremendously crucial issue of the growth of private regulation of labor standards in the context of global supply chains. In particular, the author states that Multinational Corporations (MNCs) are somewhat "under pressure" to adopt private regulatory initiatives, with dominant aim the fastest possible addressing of unsatisfactory working conditions in the factories of the global supply chain.

Steen Knudsen argues that a significant part of the literature attempts to methodically delve into issues concerning both the driving forces and the results of these control and monitoring systems.

Regrettably, however, the conclusion drawn is that this literature mainly refers to large firms, somehow ignoring the truly remarkable growing integration of SMEs within the global supply chains. This issue is particularly sensitive, although over the years, the notability of SMEs is constantly becoming more pronounced within the global literature context.

Apart from that, Steen Knudsen argues that literature on corporate social responsibility in terms of SMEs mainly focuses on domestic initiatives rather than global challenges. That particular article concentrates on the Business for Social Compliance Initiative (BSCI) and attempts a thorough analysis of the positions of private actors who seek and provide private arrangements, as well as those of specific enterprises which are regarded as the targets of these plans.

Furthermore, the author points to the fact that as the BSCI has increased its members (and also its particular noteworthiness in our opinion), Multinational Corporations are more and more asking SMEs to meet BSCI requirements in the context of global supply chains, even if this proves to be practically impossible for more than a few smaller businesses.

Finally, Bönte and Nielen (2011) meticulously focus on concepts such as product innovation, credit constraints and trade credit. In the context of this specific article, the two authors attempt an attention-grabbing study with regard to the link between innovation and commercial credit.

These authors emphatically point out that despite the fact that the concept of trade credit held a top position in the literature on economic and financial affairs (at the time the article was authored), its link to innovation was slightly neglected.

Furthermore, they argue that the possibility of using trade credit is more prominent in innovative SMEs than in non-innovative ones due to credit constraints. In addition to that, business partners are highly probable to have specific incentives in order to provide trade credit, especially to SMEs that apply innovations as far as their products are concerned.

We realize, as in other cases examined, that this article indeed remains up to date. Times may change, the overall economic situation may be altered but a number of economic components remain stable somehow "ignoring" changes in both the sociopolitical and the economic sphere.

Bönte and Nielen conduct a systematic study of the relationship between product innovation and trade credit, examining a sample of SMEs from 15 European countries (Bulgaria, Czech Republic, Germany, Greece, Estonia, Hungary, Ireland, Latvia, Lithuania, Poland, Portugal, Romania, Slovakia, Slovenia and Spain). The econometric analysis (into which we will however not delve) confirms the positive relationship between innovation and trade credit.

In other words, innovative SMEs are more likely to use trade credit than others. What is particularly important, though, is that the impact of this innovation becomes statistically significant only if SMEs report that access to finance or its cost are obstacles to business operation or development.

Therefore, always according to the authors, results actually reveal the notability of commercial credit as a source of short-term external financing for innovative SMEs facing certain credit constraints.

In general, competition policy is a fundamental part of the internal market. Hence, its rational operation can effectively contribute to the economic prosperity of the Union and its citizens (European Commission/Competition, 2015; Vasileiou, 2013a, 2014a, 2017b and 2017c).

The Union's numerous positive steps in recent years have actually proved that economic recovery, coupled with the fight against unemployment, can indeed be regarded as achievable goals, as far as, of course, systematic efforts continue at the same pace (Alexiou, 2001; Bambra and Eikemo, 2009; Bartolomew et al., 1995; Blanchflower and Shadforth, 2009; Brine, 2002; Calmfors, 2001; Christodoulakis and Mamatzakis, 2009; Coombes and Raybould, 2004; Daveri et al., 2000; Dieckhoff, 2011; Ederveen et al., 2007; European Commission, 2016; European Commission, 2017; European Union/Competition, 2017; Feld, 2005; Fialová and Schneider, 2009; Fragoulis et al., 2004; Gobbin and Van Aarle, 2001; Heinrich and Hildebrand, 2005; Janáčková, 1998; Kazamaki Ottersten, 2004; Kinsella and Kinsella, 2011; Kogan, 2004; Lipsmeyer and Zhu, 2011; Mahler et al., 2000; Newell and Pastore, 2006; Núñez and Livanos, 2010; Öster and Agell, 2007; Overman et al., 2002; Palazuelos-Martinez, 2007; Pelagidis and Mitsopoulos, 2014; Petrongolo and Pissarides, 2008; Pollmann-Schult and Büchel, 2005; Pratschke, 1981; Scott and Kelleher, 1996; Smith, 2011; Stanef, 2012; Stewart, 2005; Sweeney, 1994; Tatsiramos, 2009; Vasileiou, 2013a, 2014a, 2017b and 2017c; Vintrová, 2004; Walsh, 2000; Welbers, 2011; Zamfir, 2011).

Through a satisfactory competition policy, the EU is attempting a continuous effort to provide quality goods and services at more affordable prices (European Commission/Competition, 2015; Vasileiou, 2013a, 2014a, 2017b and 2017c).

The Commission has devoted itself to a functional (and indeed effective in our opinion, at least for the time being) mobilization of specific tools and the necessary market expertise in order for them to sufficiently contribute to the Union's jobs, growth and investment agenda, including in areas such as the energy union, the digital single market, industrial policy, financial services and the incessant fight against tax evasion, which has been plaguing more than a few member states (European Commission/Competition, 2015; Vasileiou, 2013a, 2014a, 2017b and 2017c).

The usefulness that becomes a necessity for an efficient European competition policy lies in the fact that it can bring more than a few noteworthy advantages, such as (in addition to the aforementioned low prices and improved quality) business innovation and a wider choice for consumers. Furthermore, special attention must be paid to the fact that a healthy competition within the Union significantly strengthens European companies as far as their survival in terms of the thorny path of global competition is concerned (European Commission/Competition, 2015; Vasileiou, 2013a, 2014a, 2017b and 2017c).

According to official EU data, its primary aims are a) the functional promotion of market liberalization, b) the war against monopolies and c) the detailed scrutiny of both state aid and mergers (Europa, 2017; European Commission, 2016; European Commission, 2017; European Commission/Jobs, 2016; European Union/Competition, 2017; Vasileiou, 2013a, 2014a, 2017b and 2017c).

If violations in terms of competition rules take place in only one country, then national competition authorities are usually in charge. However, due to globalization and the internal market growth, the effects of illegal practices are in many cases felt in several other countries both inside and outside the Union. This should be a matter of particular concern, but through our research we can conclude that the EU has already taken swift action (European Commission, 2016; European Commission, 2017; Vasileiou, 2013a, 2014a, 2017b and 2017c).

In particular, the European Commission normally manages to satisfactorily deal with such trans-EU cases by conducting specific investigations, taking binding decisions and imposing fines. Incontrovertibly, the Commission keeps strengthening the Union's competition rules in the context of a functional cooperation with member states' national competition authorities (European Commission, 2016; European Commission, 2017; European Union/Competition, 2017).

These authorities operate in all member states without exception and are responsible for the effective enforcement of

EU competition law, practically possessing the same powers as the Commission (Europa, 2017; European Commission, 2016; European Commission, 2017; European Commission/Jobs, 2016; Vasileiou, 2013a, 2014a, 2017b and 2017c).

According always to official Commission figures of 2016, since 2007, national competition authorities have successfully accomplished the proper application of the Union's competition rules in approximately 570 cases, which is indeed a remarkable feature (European Commission, 2016; European Union/ Competition, 2017).

Information exchange[1] between these authorities and the Commission takes place through the European Competition Network (ECN). Additionally, we must not forget that national courts are also capable of deciding whether and to what extent a certain agreement adequately complies with the Union's competition law (European Commission, 2016; European Commission, 2017; European Union/Competition, 2017).

Any agreement that results in an unintentional or deliberate restriction of competition is called "anticompetitive" and is subject to specific sanctions. A classic example is the cartels. Enterprises participating in a cartel conduct special agreements in order not to compete with each other or agree the selling prices of their products (European Commission, 2016; European Union/Competition, 2017; Vasileiou, 2013a, 2014a, 2017b and 2017c).

---

1. *As regards the best possible implementation of the Union's competition rules.*

We underline that the participation in a cartel[2] practically provides companies with a way of shielding themselves from the various pressures of competitors on price reductions, new products' launching and quality improvement. It goes without saying that the result is outstandingly negative for consumers who are "forced" to pay more for lower quality. Indubitably, such a fact is extremely unpleasant and painful, especially in times of economic crisis (Europa, 2017; European Commission, 2016; European Commission/Jobs, 2016; Vasileiou, 2013a, 2014a, 2017b and 2017c).

It is totally reasonable for every EU citizen to expect immediate action by the Union in order for such dishonest practices to be prevented. Indeed, we are able to confirm that the Union is characterized by the ability to effectively impose its powers.

Under EU competition law, cartels are considered to be illegal and the Commission imposes heavy fines on the companies involved in them. The question that arises is whether it is easy to actually discover the cartels (European Commission, 2016; European Commission, 2017; European Union/Competition, 2017).

Towards this direction the Commission follows the so-called "leniency" policy, under which the companies involved in the cartel and admit their involvement with adequate proof exempt partially or completely from the fine the Commission would otherwise impose on them (European Commission, 2016; European Commission, 2017; European Union/Competition, 2017).

---

2. *For the control of prices and the market sharing between businesses.*

In addition to that, enterprises that admit their participation in a cartel can in a sense "compromise" with the Commission. This way, not only the issue closes faster but also the Commission manages to save resources. Enterprises which finally settle actually pay a reduced fine, which is an absolutely critical parameter for them (Europa, 2017; European Commission, 2016; European Commission/Jobs, 2016; European Union/ Competition, 2017).

In particular, agreements are regarded as "anticompetitive" in the cases where participants reach an agreement a) to fix prices, b) to share customers or markets, c) to limit production and d) to fix resale prices[3] (Europa, 2017; European Commission, 2016; European Commission, 2017; European Commission/ Jobs, 2016; Vasileiou, 2013a, 2014a, 2017b and 2017c).

Nonetheless, in a number of cases, an agreement may be allowed if A) it is not concluded between competitors, B) it is characterized by more positive rather than negative effects, C) it involves companies with a small combined market share and D) it is essential a) for the development of new products, b) to substantially improve products or services and c) for the discovery of new and more satisfactory methods to make products available to consumers (Europa, 2017; European Commission, 2016; European Commission, 2017; European Commission/Jobs, 2016; European Union/Competition, 2017; Vasileiou, 2013a, 2014a, 2017b and 2017c).

---

3. *Between a producer and his distributors.*

The abuse of a dominant position is an issue of paramount importance, characterized by various multidimensional implications. Under certain circumstances, a tremendously powerful firm in a particular market may cause damage to competition (Europa, 2017; European Commission, 2016; European Commission, 2017; European Commission/Jobs, 2016; European Union/Competition, 2017).

This happens when such an enterprise engages in a systematic struggle to push its competitors out of the market. Incontrovertibly, these actions lead to a reduction or even elimination of competition and deeply affect consumers who end up with a small variety of options at increased prices (Europa, 2017; European Commission, 2016; European Commission, 2017; European Commission/Jobs, 2016; European Union/ Competition, 2017).

Apart from that, emphasis is placed on the fact that enterprises abuse their dominant position even when they a) charge unreasonably high prices b) "oblige" consumers to purchase a product which is artificially linked to another product of high demand, which helps to ensure that there are no alternatives for either or both product types[4], c) make the sale of a particular product conditional on the sale of another, d) refuse to deal with specific customers or providing special discounts to others who make most or all of their purchases from that particular (dominant) company and e) sell at artificially low prices to

---

4. *Distortion of competition.*

reduce or even completely eliminate competition from the market (European Commission, 2016; Vasileiou, 2013a, 2014a, 2017b and 2017c).

The (often neuralgic) issue of mergers is another crucial factor in the wider context of competitiveness and the numerous attempts towards the highly desirable economic recovery (European Commission, 2016; Vasileiou, 2013a, 2014a, 2017b and 2017c).

According to the Commission, mergers need to be cleared at European level in order for companies which are active in more than one member state to be "allowed" to successfully obtain clearance for their merger Europe-wide in one go. Such a component deserves special attention for quite a few reasons (European Commission, 2016; Vasileiou, 2013a, 2014a, 2017b and 2017c).

The Commission conducts a systematic investigation of any merger of companies, the turnovers of which exceed certain thresholds. It is worth noting that below these thresholds, mergers can be examined by the national competition authorities (European Commission, 2016; European Commission, 2017; Vasileiou, 2013a, 2014a, 2017b and 2017c).

Emphasis is placed on the fact that the rules apply to all mergers, irrespective of their headquarters, registered office, production facilities and activities. The Commission can examine mergers referred to it by the national competition authorities or the merging companies, while, sometimes, it can refer a case to a national competition authority (European Commission, 2016; European Commission, 2017; Vasileiou, 2013a, 2014a, 2017b and 2017c).

In the cases where a) the merger significantly weakens competition in the Union via (for instance) the reinforcement or the creation of a dominant "player", or b) the merging parties are considered to be foremost competitors, then that suggested merger can indeed be prohibited (Europa, 2017; European Commission, 2016; European Commission, 2017; European Commission/Jobs, 2016; European Union/Competition, 2017).

In a number of countries, services of paramount importance such as post, energy, transport, telecommunications and water are still controlled by public authorities (European Commission, 2016; European Commission, 2017; European Union/ Competition, 2017; Vasileiou, 2013a, 2014a, 2017b and 2017c).

It must also be mentioned that the governments of the Union's member states can entrust the responsibility of the provision of certain public services to specific companies, always subject to the condition that the rights, duties and financial compensation of these companies will definitely comply with state aid rules. Such a detail indubitably calls for particular attention (Europa, 2017; European Commission, 2016; European Commission, 2017; European Commission/Jobs, 2016; Vasileiou, 2013a, 2014a, 2017b and 2017c).

It is necessary to add that in a number of cases these services are liberalized. There, the Commission takes the necessary measures to ensure that everyone can benefit from these services even in areas where their provision is deemed to be unprofitable (Europa, 2017; European Commission, 2016; European Commission, 2017; European Commission/Jobs, 2016; European Union/Competition, 2017).

Furthermore, it is literally "compulsory" to guarantee that the liberalization procedure takes place through a specific method which does not confer unfair advantages on the company which previously held the monopoly (Europa, 2017; European Commission, 2016; European Commission, 2017; European Commission/Jobs, 2016; Vasileiou, 2013a, 2014a, 2017b and 2017c).

Another highly significant element is the fact that sometimes the Commission can actually give its approval to a company, in order for the latter to have a monopoly. Typical examples are cases where outstandingly expensive infrastructures are needed (natural monopolies), or where the ensuring of a certain public service is considered to be absolutely necessary (European Commission, 2016; European Commission, 2017; European Union/Competition, 2017; Vasileiou, 2013a, 2014a, 2017b and 2017c).

Nevertheless, we must stress that a) natural monopolies must make their infrastructure available to all users without exception, b) monopoly companies have to be capable of sufficiently proving that they treat other companies fairly and c) the various profits arising from the provision of a public service cannot be used to subsidize commercial operations, which would lead to lower prices compared to those of the competitors (Europa, 2017; European Commission, 2016; European Commission/Jobs, 2016; European Union/Competition, 2017; Vasileiou, 2013a, 2014a, 2017b and 2017c).

We strongly believe that the efforts in general of large firms to exploit their bargaining power[5], in order to manage to impose conditions that would prevent their customers or suppliers to transact with competitors, is clearly contrary to the Union's philosophy (Europa, 2017; European Union/Competition, 2017; European Commission/Jobs, 2016; European Commission, 2017; Vasileiou, 2013a, 2014a, 2017b and 2017c).

Wherever such phenomena occur, the European Commission, without further delay, imposes fines since such practices are proven to lead to both a smaller variety for consumers and higher prices (European Union/Competition, 2017; European Commission, 2017; Vasileiou, 2013a, 2014a, 2017b and 2017c).

These actions of the Union clearly demonstrate its determination to protect small enterprises at all costs. It is unambiguous that governments can assist firms experiencing a difficult phase as far as the latter prove that they can indeed become profitable and maintain or create jobs (Europa, 2017; European Commission, 2016; European Commission, 2017; European Commission/Jobs, 2016; European Union/Competition, 2017; Vasileiou, 2013a, 2014a, 2017b and 2017c).

---

5. *In the context of their dealings with smaller enterprises.*

Nevertheless, governments are explicitly forbidden to support firms in trouble that are clearly not probable to ever become viable (Europa, 2017; European Commission, 2016; European Commission, 2017; European Commission/Jobs, 2016; European Union/Competition, 2017; Vasileiou, 2013a, 2014a, 2017b and 2017c).

As usual, exceptions to the rules incontrovertibly exist and concern a) regional development projects, b) companies that cooperate in order to accomplish the functional development of single technical standards for the entire market, c) specific initiatives related to research and innovation, which is an absolutely vital component for the EU future and d) smaller companies which cooperate so as to increase their competitiveness vis-à-vis the larger ones (Europa, 2017; European Commission, 2017; European Commission/Jobs, 2016; European Union/ Competition, 2017; Vasileiou, 2013a, 2014a, 2017b and 2017c).

From the entire range of the abovementioned issues, we are in position to conclude that the Union is irrefutably conducting numerous systematic and consistent attempts towards a) the promotion of constructive competition b) the protection of healthy businesses and c) combating unemployment. In the future we look forward to even more positive results (Alexiou, 2001; Bambra and Eikemo, 2009; Bartolomew et al., 1995; Blanchflower and Shadforth, 2009; Brine, 2002; Calmfors, 2001; Christodoulakis and Mamatzakis, 2009; Coombes and Raybould, 2004; Daveri et al., 2000; Dieckhoff, 2011;

Ederveen et al., 2007; Europa, 2017; European Commission, 2016; European Commission/Jobs, 2016; European Union/ Competition, 2017; Feld, 2005; Fialová and Schneider, 2009; Fragoulis et al., 2004; Gobbin and Van Aarle, 2001; Heinrich and Hildebrand, 2005; Janáčková, 1998; Kazamaki Ottersten, 2004; Kinsella and Kinsella, 2011; Kogan, 2004; Lipsmeyer and Zhu, 2011; Mahler et al., 2000; Newell and Pastore, 2006; Núñez and Livanos, 2010; Öster and Agell, 2007; Overman et al., 2002; Palazuelos-Martinez, 2007; Pelagidis and Mitsopoulos, 2014; Petrongolo and Pissarides, 2008; Pollmann-Schult and Büchel, 2005; Pratschke, 1981; Scott and Kelleher, 1996; Smith, 2011; Stanef, 2012; Stewart, 2005; Sweeney, 1994; Tatsiramos, 2009; Vasileiou, 2013a, 2014a, 2017b and 2017c; Vintrová, 2004; Walsh, 2000; Welbers, 2011; Zamfir, 2011).

In the next chapter, we attempt to scrupulously examine the Union's institutions in charge of competition rules. In particular, we meticulously concentrate on the responsibilities of the European Parliament, the Council of the EU, the European Commission, the European Economic and Social Committee and the Committee of the Regions.

Special emphasis is placed on: a) the two committees of the Parliament (the Committee on the Internal Market and Consumer Protection and the Committee on Economic and Monetary Affairs), b) the Competitiveness Council, c) the European Economic and Social Committee's Section for the Single Market, Production and Consumption and d) the Commission for Economic Policy of the Committee of the Regions.

CHAPTER 2

EUROPEAN UNION INSTITUTIONS IN THE CONTEXT OF COMPETITION RULES

In the previous chapter, we attempted a methodical clarification in terms of the "competition rules" concept. We outlined the principal findings from the existing literature, cited the foremost scholars who have successfully dealt with these issues and rigorously examined more than a few fundamental parameters.

Now it is time to go a bit further, carefully focusing on the institutions involved in the procedures and in a sense shape the overall framework of competition policies by actually encouraging the ceaseless promotion of undistorted competition within the Union context.

It is unambiguous that fair competition leads to an infinitely more efficient and profitable system which clearly supports healthy enterprises, combats unemployment and continuously promotes economic growth (Alexiou, 2001; Bambra and Eikemo, 2009; Bartolomew et al., 1995; Blanchflower and Shadforth, 2009; Brine, 2002; Calmfors, 2001; Christodoulakis and Mamatzakis, 2009; Coombes and Raybould, 2004; Daveri et al., 2000; Dieckhoff, 2011; Ederveen et al., 2007; European

Commission, 2016; European Union/Competition, 2017; Feld, 2005; Fialová and Schneider, 2009; Fragoulis et al., 2004; Gobbin and Van Aarle, 2001; Heinrich and Hildebrand, 2005; Janáčková, 1998; Kazamaki Ottersten, 2004; Kinsella and Kinsella, 2011; Kogan, 2004; Lipsmeyer and Zhu, 2011; Mahler et al., 2000; Newell and Pastore, 2006; Núñez and Livanos, 2010; Öster and Agell, 2007; Overman et al., 2002; Palazuelos-Martinez, 2007; Pelagidis and Mitsopoulos, 2014; Petrongolo and Pissarides, 2008; Pollmann-Schult and Büchel, 2005; Pratschke, 1981; Scott and Kelleher, 1996; Smith, 2011; Stanef, 2012; Stewart, 2005; Sweeney, 1994; Tatsiramos, 2009; Vasileiou, 2013a, 2014a, 2017b and 2017c; Vintrová, 2004; Walsh, 2000; Welbers, 2011; Zamfir, 2011).

The Union's institutions as far as competition rules are concerned are the European Parliament, the Council of the EU, the European Commission, the European Economic and Social Committee and the Committee of the Regions.

The starting point of our analysis is the European Parliament's Committee on the Internal Market and Consumer Protection (IMCO). IMCO is in charge of both the legislative oversight and the detailed examination of Union rules on the free movement of goods and services, customs policy, the free movement of professionals, standardization and the consumers' economic interests (European Commission, 2017; European Parliament/Committees/IMCO, 2017; Vasileiou, 2013a, 2014a, 2017b and 2017c).

The European Parliament's Committee on Economic and Monetary Affairs (ECON) plays its own distinct role as it is in charge of a) the Economic and Monetary Union (EMU), b) the international financial system, c) competition and taxation, d) the efficacious and rapid regulation in terms of financial services and e) the free movement of capital and payments (European Commission, 2017; European Parliament/Committees/ECON, 2017; Vasileiou, 2013a, 2014a, 2017b and 2017c).

Both IMCO and ECON are widely regarded as two of Parliament's most multifarious committees, characterized by numerous responsibilities of paramount noteworthiness. Such a remarkable element demonstrates for one more time the Parliament's vital role within the wider context of the abovementioned issues.

The Competitiveness Council (COMPET) is in charge of a) stimulating and strengthening competitiveness in the Union and b) substantially supporting and increasing growth. It is not difficult to realize the high degree complexity of these goals, which actually set out the designing of a wide range of fundamental objectives both for the present and the future. Practically, the Council deals with industry, the internal market, space and research and innovation (European Commission, 2017; European Council/Council of the European Union, 2017; Vasileiou, 2013a, 2014a, 2017b and 2017c).

In the context of the Competitiveness Council, according always to the agenda, ministers of all member states, in charge of the economy, the industry, trade, space and research and innovation are "brought together". Relevant European Commissioners also take part in the meetings. At least four meetings are held each year, and such an element indeed proves its momentousness (European Commission, 2017; European Council/Council of the European Union, 2017; Vasileiou, 2013a, 2014a, 2017b and 2017c).

More specifically, in terms of the industrial sector, the Council is characterized by a fairly successful combination of a horizontal approach (the primary objective of which is the effective and functional integration of industrial policy issues into all other relevant Union policies) with a sector-specific one (European Commission, 2017; European Council/Council of the European Union, 2017; Vasileiou, 2013a, 2014a, 2017b and 2017c).

Apart from that, the Council is constantly attempting to sufficiently enhance business environment with a special focus on SMEs which, as we have already mentioned, are a pivotal aspect for the Union's economic recovery (Europa, 2017; European Commission, 2017; European Commission/Jobs, 2016; European Council/Council of the European Union, 2017; Vasileiou, 2013a, 2014a, 2017b and 2017c).

Simultaneously, it co-legislates on certain measures for these businesses, such as a) the effective promotion and encouragement of innovation b) the cutting of (the almost always problematic) red tape and c) the significant enhancement as regards the coveted access to funding (an absolutely vital component particularly in times of economic crisis) (European Commission, 2017; European Council/Council of the European Union, 2017; Vasileiou, 2013a, 2014a, 2017b and 2017c).

As far as the internal market is concerned, the Council as law-maker methodically operates towards the rapid removal of all barriers and related obstacles which hamper the smooth cross-border flow of labor, services, capital and products (European Commission, 2017; European Council/Council of the European Union, 2017; Vasileiou, 2013a, 2014a, 2017b and 2017c).

Finally, in terms of the area of research, innovation and space, the Council's dominant objective is to provide a satisfactory reinforcement of the scientific and technological base of European industry, with a view to promoting its international competitiveness which may, inter alia, result in a higher degree of growth and employment (Europa, 2017; European Commission, 2017; European Commission/Jobs, 2016; European Council/Council of the European Union, 2017; Vasileiou, 2013a, 2014a, 2017b and 2017c).

We must underline the outstandingly important fact that the Council closely cooperates with the European Space Agency on the proper development of the European space policy (European Commission, 2017; European Council/Council of the European Union, 2017; Vasileiou, 2013a, 2014a, 2017b, 2017c and 2017e).

As regards the Commission, it goes without saying that it has been devoted to a continuous and persistent struggle in order for national measures (taken so as to satisfactorily confront the economic and financial crisis) not to lead to the undesirable (in numerous respects) distortion of competition, but to take the wider European context seriously into account (Europa, 2017; European Commission, 2016; European Commission/ Jobs, 2016; European Union/Competition, 2017; Vasileiou, 2013a, 2014a, 2017b and 2017c).

In the previous chapter, we referred somewhat superficially to quite a few of the Commission's actions regarding competition rules. In this chapter, we attempt a more scrupulous analysis towards a better understanding.

It is true that the Union's general rules on the particularly neuralgic area of government support actually prevent governments from competing with each other in terms of which will be able to further "strengthen" its own companies at the expense of their healthy competitors (European Commission, 2016; European Union/Competition, 2017; Vasileiou, 2013a, 2014a, 2017b and 2017c).

Nevertheless, the Commission issued certain temporary rules towards a satisfactory support for banks, in order for a number of governments to be able to effectively cope with the crisis[6]. Apart from the banks, the Commission adopted temporary rules for companies in order for governments to be provided with facilitation in terms of the thorny issue of credit squeeze (Europa, 2017; European Commission, 2016; European

---

6. *Under these rules, banks cannot accept public support unless they take measures themselves in order to adequately resolve their problems.*

Commission/Jobs, 2016; European Union/Competition, 2017; Vasileiou, 2013a, 2014a, 2017b and 2017c).

In particular, it allowed governments to make use of the following (tremendously significant) measures: a) export credit insurance, b) facilitation (always to a feasible extent) in terms of the access of companies to finance, c) subsidized loans[7] and d) state guarantees for loans at a reduced premium (European Commission, 2016; European Union/Competition, 2017; Vasileiou, 2013a, 2014a, 2017b and 2017c).

At this point, we consider it necessary to focus on the tremendously significant investigative powers of the Commission. In order to be more precise, whenever the Commission takes the decision to investigate possible anti-competitive practices, its officials have the following rights: a) to enter any company premises, means of transport, or land, b) to carry out in-depth examinations of business books and miscellaneous business records and take copies or extracts from them, c) to ask any representative or staff member specific details and explanations regarding documents or facts related to the purpose of the inspection and to record the answers and d) to seal any business premises, as well as any records or books for the period and to the extent necessary for that particular inspection (European Commission, 2016; European Commission, 2017; Vasileiou, 2013a, 2014a, 2017b and 2017c).

---

7. *Especially with regard to eco-friendly products.*

Another burning issue is the method according to which the Commission reaches decisions on which support is allowed. More specifically, the Commission is obliged to rigorously examine the following important parameters: a) whether state authorities have actually provided support[8], b) if such support can practically affect trade between member states, c) whether a distortion of competition has already occurred or is probable to occur in the future and d) whether the support is regarded as "selective"[9] (European Commission, 2016; European Union/Competition, 2017; Vasileiou, 2013a, 2014a, 2017b and 2017c).

If the abovementioned parameters apply, the Commission is literally "obliged" to prohibit the support, unless there is sufficient evidence that it is indeed compatible with the internal market (European Commission, 2016; European Union/ Competition, 2017; Vasileiou, 2013a, 2014a, 2017b and 2017c).

The question arising is precisely how government support is being monitored. Generally speaking, the governments of the Union must inform the Commission about both planned subsidies and miscellaneous forms of support before granting them. It is worth mentioning that out of the total notified support, following a specific preliminary assessment,

---

8. *In the form of a) holdings in companies, b) guarantees, c) grants, interest and tax relief, and d) the provision of services and goods on preferential terms.*

9. *We mean if it provides an advantage on certain companies, companies in specific regions, or parts of industries. We persist in the fact that both employment legislation and general tax measures do not constitute selective support. Such a crucial component always deserves special attention.*

the Commission finally approves approximately 85% (European Commission, 2016; European Commission, 2017; European Union/Competition, 2017).

Whenever a formal investigation is deemed necessary, this is announced both in the Official Journal of the EU and on the Commission's online register of state aid policies. Interested parties have the opportunity to submit comments, while the Commission carries out an intensive and highly systematic study of the case before reaching a final decision (European Commission, 2016; European Union/Competition, 2017).

In addition to that, the Commission examines in detail support for which it was not officially informed but instead discovered a) from the media, b) following complaints by individuals or companies, or c) by conducting its own investigation (European Commission, 2016; European Union/Competition, 2017; Vasileiou, 2013a, 2014a, 2017b and 2017c).

What is more, it is stressed that unless the Commission concludes that support is regarded as compatible with the Union law and the principles of fair competition, it requires from the authorities not only to discontinue its granting but also the rapid retrieve of its already granted part (European Commission, 2016; European Commission, 2017; European Union/Competition, 2017; Vasileiou, 2013a, 2014a, 2017b and 2017c).

The scoreboard regarding the Commission's state aid is of paramount notability due to the fact that it satisfactorily provides statistics on both the total amount and the specific type of support allocated by each member state (European Commission, 2016; European Commission, 2017; European Union/Competition, 2017).

Special emphasis is placed on the fact that from January 2016, citizens in all member states can actually discover information on subsidies over €500,000 through the website of the Directorate-General for Competition. As we can easily understand, the advantages resulting from such facility are more than a few (European Commission, 2016; European Union/ Competition, 2017).

According to the abovementioned scoreboard, the majority of support granted to individual companies and industries in the past is now unambiguously redirected on actions in the common interest of the Union, which is an absolutely remarkable fact that can lead to a more optimistic future (European Commission, 2016; European Commission, 2017; European Union/Competition, 2017; Vasileiou, 2013a, 2014a, 2017b and 2017c).

Furthermore, the entire range regarding the Union's investigations in terms of competition issues, apart from goods, cover both professions and services, including financial ones[10], which is a parameter of tremendous importance especially nowadays (Europa, 2017; European Commission, 2016; European Commission, 2017; European Commission/Jobs, 2016; European Union/Competition, 2017).

---

10. *For example credit cards and retail banking.*

With regard to troubled enterprises, the Commission conducts an outstandingly systematic control in terms of the amount of assistance provided to various businesses by governments of member states (European Union/Competition, 2017; Vasileiou, 2013a, 2014a, 2017b and 2017c).

These state aids include, inter alia, a) specific tax breaks, b) certain government guarantees which manage to improve the credit rating of a company over its competitors, c) grants and loans and d) the provision of goods and services at preferential rates (European Union/Competition, 2017; Vasileiou, 2013a, 2014a, 2017b and 2017c).

At this point, we will meticulously delve into the ECN's foremost responsibilities. The ECN plays a key role as far as the continuous promotion of healthy competition is concerned. In particular, the Commission and national competition authorities in all member states without a single exception engage in a satisfactory cooperation with each other via the ECN (European Commission/Competition/ECN, 2017; European Commission/Competition/ECN/Cooperation, 2016; European Commission/Competition/ECN/Details, 2012).

We would argue that such a practice actually leads to the materialization of a particularly efficacious mechanism to counter companies that engage in specific cross-border practices that restrict competition. As the European competition rules are applied by ECN members, the ECN generously provides the precise means to guarantee their consistent, functional and, above all, sufficient application. This element is of paramount significance and we can easily understand why (European Commission/Competition/ECN, 2017; European Commission/Competition/ECN/Cooperation, 2016; European Commission/Competition/ECN/Details, 2012).

What is more, via the ECN, competition authorities can inform each other on proposed decisions and also receive suggestions and comments from other competition authorities. Such cooperation is particularly constructive since it practically enables the ECN to "allow" competition authorities to concentrate their experiences towards the desirable identification of best practices (European Commission/Competition/ECN, 2017; European Commission/Competition/ECN/Cooperation, 2016; European Commission/Competition/ECN/Details, 2012).

It is worth mentioning that the foundations of ECN operation are laid out in the "Commission Notice on cooperation within the Network of Competition Authorities" and the "Joint Statement of the Council and the Commission on the Functioning of the Network of Competition Authorities" (European Commission/Competition/ECN, 2017; European Commission/Competition/ECN/Cooperation, 2016; European Commission/Competition/ECN/Details, 2012).

The cooperation between the Commission and the competition authorities of member states via the ECN is based on a) the proper coordination of investigations where absolutely necessary and an effective mutual assistance,

b) the direct information between them on new cases and envisaged enforcement decisions, c) the operational exchange of evidence and miscellaneous information and d) constructive discussions on numerous issues of common interest (European Commission/Competition/ECN, 2017; European Commission/Competition/ECN/Cooperation, 2016; European Commission/Competition/ECN/Details, 2012).

The ECN's truly multidimensional role is unambiguously demonstrated by the fact that within its wider context, discussions on competition problems and the best possible promotion of a common approach indeed take place (European Commission/Competition/ECN, 2017; European Commission/Competition/ECN/Cooperation, 2016; European Commission/Competition/ECN/Details, 2012).

In terms of these discussions, experts in a a wide range of sectors including energy, banking, securities, insurance, professional services, food, pharmaceuticals, healthcare, the environment, motor vehicles, telecommunications, media, railways, abuse of dominant positions and IT and information and communication participate. Moreover, Competition Chief Economists can also take part in discussions (European Commission/Competition/ECN, 2017; European Commission/Competition/ECN/Cooperation, 2016; European Commission/Competition/ECN/Details, 2012).

Special attention must be paid to the fact that ECN members have managed to establish an outstandingly significant EU

Merger Working Group. Via the latter, members perform a constructive cooperation and a fruitful exchange of best practices within the particularly neuralgic area of merger control (European Commission/Competition/ECN, 2017; European Commission/Competition/ECN/Cooperation, 2016; European Commission/Competition/ECN/Details, 2012).

This Working Group was established in Brussels in 2010 and comprises representatives from the Commission and the national authorities of the Union in charge of merger review (NCAs), together with observers from the NCAs of the European Economic Area. We argue that the dominant pursuit of that specific Working Group is the efficient encouragement and promotion of an increased cooperation and convergence among EU merger jurisdictions (European Commission/Competition/ECN, 2017; European Commission/Competition/ECN/Cooperation, 2016; European Commission/Competition/ECN/Details, 2012).

In other words, the Working Group is engaged in a systematic effort in order for merger issues with a cross-border impact to be sufficiently enhanced. Simultaneously, it seeks to find the best possible solutions, always taking existing legal frameworks into account and drawing from the experience and the practices of agencies (European Commission/Competition/ECN, 2017; European Commission/Competition/ECN/Cooperation, 2016; European Commission/Competition/ECN/Details, 2012).

We highlight the fact that the (admittedly) extensive powers of the Commission to investigate and bring to an end violations in terms of the Union's competition rules are subject to judicial review by the European Courts (European Commission, 2016; European Commission, 2017; European Union/Competition, 2017; Vasileiou, 2013a, 2014a, 2017b and 2017c).

It is true that both EU governments and companies often lodge and in a number of cases actually succeed in terms of appeals against certain Commission decisions. This is another attention-grabbing parameter in the context of activities in general, in order for competition rules to be adequately followed (European Commission, 2016; European Commission, 2017; European Union/Competition, 2017; Vasileiou, 2013a, 2014a, 2017b and 2017c).

According to Commission's estimations of 2016, in 2015 the consumers' benefits from just the decisions according to which the Commission was banning cartels ranged between €999 million and €1.49 bn. What is more, the Commission imposed fines of €364,531,000 related to cartel decisions (European Commission, 2016; European Union/Competition, 2017).

Incontrovertibly, these data provide us with proof that EU does not tolerate any phenomena which are highly probable to "infect" healthy competition. This practice increases, among other things, the Union's solvency degree vis-à-vis its citizens. Such a relationship of trust is irrefutably fundamental especially in the present difficult times.

The European Economic and Social Committee's Section for the Single Market, Production and Consumption (INT) is also in charge of a wide range of key issues.

Its tasks include a complex set of policy areas that are linked in a multifunctional range of policy areas, which are connected with competition, industry, SMEs, services and social economy enterprises. Concomitantly, it discusses and adopts opinions on a) consumer protection, b) research and innovation and c) emerging economic trends[11] (Europa, 2017; European Commission, 2017; European Commission/Jobs, 2016; European Economic and Social Committee, 2017; Vasileiou, 2013a, 2014a, 2017b and 2017c).

We underline the fact that, with regard to issues of primary noteworthiness to the Single Market, the Section meticulously holds public hearings aiming at the systematic consultation with as many civil society organizations as possible. Furthermore, it is worth mentioning that since 1999 the Section has been organizing every year the outstandingly noteworthy "European Consumer Day" (European Commission, 2017; European Economic and Social Committee, 2017; Vasileiou, 2013a, 2014a, 2017b and 2017c).

Apart from that, the Section also has a Single Market Observatory which undertakes an outstandingly detailed monitoring of developments within the Single Market context, proposing enhancements and solutions to the problems

---

11. *In particular, the extremely notable collaborative economy and Single Market policies in general, which are regarded as tremendously essential components for both the present and the future.*

(European Commission, 2017; European Economic and Social Committee, 2017; Vasileiou, 2013a, 2014a, 2017b and 2017c).

The final step of our analysis is the examination of the responsibilities of the Commission for Economic Policy (ECON), which is responsible for the proper coordination of the work of the Committee of the Regions in seven of the most neuralgic areas for both the present and the future of the Union. These are a) Economic and Monetary Policy, b) Industrial Policy, c) the Internal Market, d) SME policy, e) International Trade and Tariffs, f) Competition and State aid policy and g) Economic Governance, European Semester (CoR Commissions, 2017; Europa, 2017; European Commission, 2017; European Commission/Jobs, 2016; Vasileiou, 2013a, 2014a, 2017b and 2017c).

We can indubitably observe the Union's detailed organization, which is accompanied by an unwavering will to promote the rational implementation of competition rules and to adequately protect enterprises in need, always with an emphasis on SMEs (Anton et al., 1996; Antony et al., 2008; Bönte and Nielen, 2011; Cordeiro et al., 2012; Duh et al., 2009; Dyker, 2001; Jarvis et al., 2002; Jenkins, 2006; Major, 2008; Ortiz Avram and Kühne, 2008; Parker, 1999; Perrini, 2006; Petrakos, 1996; Russo and Perrini, 2010; Russo and Tencati, 2009; Spence and Schmidpeter, 2003; Steen Knudsen, 2013; Sternberg and Arndt, 2001; Svetličič et al., 2007; Uhlaner et al., 2012; von Weltzien Heivik and Shankar, 2011).

On the basis of the abovementioned data, we can incontrovertibly argue that the Union's economic recovery is by no means utopia provided of course that specific conditions apply explicitly and firmly to all. In such a case, hopes of combating unemployment, a rapid economic reconstruction and, more generally, the emergence of a climate of prosperity in the Union (which has been a common desire and pursuit for many years) can actually become a reality (Alexiou, 2001; Bambra and Eikemo, 2009; Bartolomew et al., 1995; Blanchflower and Shadforth, 2009; Brine, 2002; Calmfors, 2001; Christodoulakis and Mamatzakis, 2009; Coombes and Raybould, 2004; Daveri et al., 2000; Dieckhoff, 2011; Ederveen et al., 2007; European Commission, 2016; European Union/Competition, 2017; Feld, 2005; Fialová and Schneider, 2009; Fragoulis et al., 2004; Gobbin and Van Aarle, 2001; Heinrich and Hildebrand, 2005; Janáčková, 1998; Kazamaki Ottersten, 2004; Kinsella and Kinsella, 2011; Kogan, 2004; Lipsmeyer and Zhu, 2011; Mahler et al., 2000; Newell and Pastore, 2006; Núñez and Livanos, 2010; Öster and Agell, 2007; Overman et al., 2002; Palazuelos-Martinez, 2007; Pelagidis and Mitsopoulos, 2014; Petrongolo and Pissarides, 2008; Pollmann-Schult and Büchel, 2005; Pratschke, 1981; Scott and Kelleher, 1996; Smith, 2011; Stanef, 2012; Stewart, 2005; Sweeney, 1994; Tatsiramos, 2009; Vasileiou, 2013a, 2014a, 2017b and 2017c; Vintrová, 2004; Walsh, 2000; Welbers, 2011; Zamfir, 2011).

The necessity to heal the wounds by such a severe crisis unambiguously underlines the tremendous usefulness of continuous and uninterrupted efforts. A rational compliance with competition rules in close connection with the incessant fight against any negative practice, can indeed serve as not only a guarantee for the future but also a functional compass towards the discovery of new ways of prosperity, development, progress, equality and social harmony.

In the following (and final) chapter, the foremost concluding remarks are being drawn. These aim at a) the most effective summary of the book's foremost points, b) the analysis of the degree of success so far, c) the identification of mistakes and d) the examination regarding future prospects.

We truly hope that the critical dimension we have brought to this study has enabled the reader to draw his personal conclusions, which may well serve as a constructive guide for further research.

CHAPTER 3

CONCLUDING REMARKS

Following the examination of a number of specific issues, we attempt to draw a number of fruitful conclusions, which in our opinion effectively summarize the main points of this book.

First of all, we remain optimistic that in the mind of the reader there should no longer be any doubt as to whether the EU really has a real interest in defining and supervising the satisfactory application of competition rules towards a fairer and more profitable enterprise activity.

Ever since its establishment, the Union's fundamental aims have been a) the promotion in terms of the liberalization of the markets, b) the "anti-monopoly" fight and c) the careful control of state aid and mergers. We strongly believe that the Union has thus far remained faithful to its initial principles, ideas and declarations.

Through our hitherto conducted research, we indubitably argue that the Union indeed combats unfair competition and acts on the basis of common interest as its history and overall philosophy dictate.

The economic crisis made things outstandingly difficult, but at the same time alerted the Union in order to review some of its key strategies and to intensify efforts for economic survival and growth. These days, the EU keeps looking to the future with optimism and we are indeed pleased to witness that its overall actions to permanently eradicate the crisis' effects in all member states without exception continue at a steady pace. We strongly believe that the Commission's priorities for the period 2015-19 perfectly reflect the general guidelines according to which the Union keeps heading towards a better future (Alexiou, 2001; Bambra and Eikemo, 2009; Bartolomew et al., 1995; Blanchflower and Shadforth, 2009; Brine, 2002; Calmfors, 2001; Christodoulakis and Mamatzakis, 2009; Coombes and Raybould, 2004; Daveri et al., 2000; Dieckhoff, 2011; Ederveen et al., 2007; European Commission, 2016; European Commission, 2017; European Union/Competition, 2017; Feld, 2005; Fialová and Schneider, 2009; Fragoulis et al., 2004; Gobbin and Van Aarle, 2001; Heinrich and Hildebrand, 2005; Janáčková, 1998; Kazamaki Ottersten, 2004; Kinsella and Kinsella, 2011; Kogan, 2004; Lipsmeyer and Zhu, 2011; Mahler et al., 2000; Newell and Pastore, 2006; Núñez and Livanos, 2010; Öster and Agell, 2007; Overman et al., 2002; Palazuelos-Martinez, 2007; Pelagidis and Mitsopoulos, 2014; Petrongolo and Pissarides, 2008; Pollmann-Schult and Büchel, 2005; Pratschke, 1981; Scott and Kelleher, 1996; Smith, 2011; Stanef, 2012; Stewart, 2005; Sweeney, 1994; Tatsiramos, 2009; Vasileiou, 2013a, 2014a, 2017b and 2017c; Vintrová, 2004; Walsh, 2000; Welbers, 2011; Zamfir, 2011).

The EU strongly advocates the efficacious protection of small businesses and the avoidance of support for troubled firms. Its design so far confirms its occasional statements on these issues, establishing an even stronger relationship of trust with its citizens. It is a common belief in the Union that the SMEs' continuous support and growth is one of the dominant elements towards a rapid economic recovery.

As we have already noticed, particularly in Chapter 1, the proper and efficient operation of SMEs is a predominant issue of research for numerous well-known scholars around the globe. The enormous variety and diversity of articles that have occasionally been published in some of the most prestigious scientific journals worldwide, conspicuously demonstrate this outstanding significance (Anton et al., 1996; Antony et al., 2008; Bönte and Nielen, 2011; Cordeiro et al., 2012; Duh et al., 2009; Dyker, 2001; Jarvis et al., 2002; Jenkins, 2006; Major, 2008; Ortiz Avram and Kühne, 2008; Parker, 1999; Perrini, 2006; Petrakos, 1996; Russo and Perrini, 2010; Russo and Tencati, 2009; Spence and Schmidpeter, 2003; Steen Knudsen, 2013; Sternberg and Arndt, 2001; Svetličič et al., 2007; Uhlaner et al., 2012; von Weltzien Heivik and Shankar, 2011).

The European Parliament, the Council of the EU, the European Commission, the European Economic and Social Committee and the Committee of the Regions are in charge of tremendously complex issues as far as competition rules are concerned. Despite the many difficulties, their work is incontrovertibly successful and this may guarantee a better future.

We imagine that the scrupulous examination of a) the two committees of the Parliament, b) the Competitiveness Council, c) the Section for the Single Market, Production and Consumption of the European Economic and Social Committee, and d) the Commission for Economic Policy of the Committee of the Regions shed light on a number of burning issues. At this particular time mistakes cost too much, so we incontrovertibly realize the increased importance of decisions and actions.

Apart from that, we hope that the critical dimension we attempted to add to our analysis succeeded in contributing to a simplification of the admittedly multidimensional spectrum of the Union's instruments and policies. Such diversity is highly probable to lead to misunderstandings and confusion, but we hope that we managed to avoid (as much as possible) ambiguities and abstruse arguments.

We are indeed in position to confirm that the Union is constantly striving to put an end to all anti-competitive practices and to protect as effectively as possible both healthy businesses and taxpayers. We irrefutably understand that the issue of healthy competition is linked not only with numerous significant policies, but also with tremendously critical social components. Apart from purely economic, the issue is also moral, since the Union is called upon to defend a number of its traditional values, such as equality, transparency and the continuous struggle for the general interest.

In order for the economic crisis to be terminated and for member states to enter into a full orbit of prosperity, healthy competition is beyond doubt one of the most important aspects. Efforts that are already taking place should in no way be stopped or reduced and we are confident that under this condition, in the near future, we will witness even more positive results.

We hope that the method of analysis on which we relied has shed light on some dark and possibly unknown to the general public aspects, while also providing the reader with impetus not only for the best possible understanding but also for further study.

The issue of competition rules could very well be described as inexhaustible, therefore a constructive and functional future research becomes more than necessary and we wholeheartedly wish this book to be a satisfactory starting point for an even more valuable research.

BIBLIOGRAPHY

Alexiou, Constantinos (2001), "Crafting a Post-Keynesian Macroeconomic Framework to Explain European Unemployment: Econometric Evidence from the European Union Countries", *Journal of Post Keynesian Economics*, 24 (1), pp. 59-80.

Anton, Ion, Danciu, Doina and Mitu, Constanta (1996), "The Role of SMEs in the Regional Redevelopment of Romania", *Eastern European Economics*, 34 (2), pp. 65-95.

Antony, J., Kumar, M. and Labib, A. (2008), "Gearing Six Sigma into UK Manufacturing SMEs: Results from a Pilot Study", *The Journal of the Operational Research Society*, 59 (4), pp. 482-493.

Bambra, C. and Eikemo, T.A. (2009), "Welfare state regimes, unemployment and health: a comparative study of the relationship between unemployment and self-reported health in 23 European countries", *Journal of Epidemiology and Community Health (1979-)*, 63 (2), pp. 92-98.

Bartolomew, David, Moore, Peter, Smith, Fred and Allin, Paul (1995), "The Measurement of Unemployment in the UK", *Journal of the Royal Statistical Society. Series A (Statistics in Society)*, 158 (3), pp. 363-417.

Blanchflower, David G. and Shadforth, Chris (2009), "Fear, Unemployment and Migration", *The Economic Journal*, 119 (535), pp. F136-F182.

Bönte, Werner and Nielen, Sebastian (2011), "Product Innovation, Credit Constraints, and Trade Credit: Evidence from a Cross-country Study", *Managerial and Decision Economics*, 32 (6), pp. 413-424.

Brine, Jacky (2002), "Further Education Participation, European Expansion and European Erasure", *British Educational Research Journal*, 28 (1), pp. 21-36.

BIBLIOGRAPHY

Calmfors, Lars (2001), "Unemployment, Labor Market Reform and Monetary Union", *Journal of Labor Economics*, 19 (2), pp. 265-289.

Christodoulakis, G.A and Mamatzakis, E.C. (2009), "Assessing the Prudence of Economic Forecasts in the EU", *Journal of Applied Econometrics*, 24 (4), pp. 583-606.

Coombes, Mike and Raybould, Simon (2004), "Finding Work in 2001: Urban-Rural Contrasts across England in Employment Rates and Local Job Availability", *Area*, 36 (2), pp. 202-222.

CoR Commissions (2017), "Commission for Economic Policy (ECON)" (in Greek), available at http://cor.europa. eu/el/activities/commissions/Pages/cor-commissions. aspx?comm=ECON (accessed on 12/11/17).

Cordeiro, JJ, Sarkis, J., Vasquez-Brust, D., Frater, L. and Dijkshoorn, J. (2012), "An evaluation of technical efficiency and managerial correlates of solid waste management by Welsh SMEs using parametric and non-parametric techniques", *The Journal of the Operational Research Society*, 63 (5), pp. 653-664.

Daveri, Francesco, Tabellini, Guido, Bentolila, Samuel and Huizinga, Harry (2000), "Unemployment, Growth and Taxation in Industrial Countries", *Economic Policy*, 15 (30), pp. 47-104.

Dieckhoff, Martina (2011), "The effect of unemployment on subsequent job quality in Europe: A comparative study of four countries", *Acta Sociologica*, 54 (3), pp. 233-249.

Duh, Mojca, Tominc, Polona and Rebernik, Miroslav (2009), "The Importance of Family Enterprises in Transition Economies: Is It Overestimated?", *Eastern European Economics*, 47 (6), pp. 22-42.

BIBLIOGRAPHY

Dyker, David A. (2001), "The Dynamic Impact on the Central-Eastern European Economies of Accession to the European Union: Social Capability and Technology Absorption", *Europe-Asia Studies*, 53 (7), pp. 1001-1021.

Ederveen, Sjef, Nahuis, Richard and Parikh, Ashok (2007), "Labour Mobility and Regional Disparities: The Role of Female Labour Participation", *Journal of Population Economics*, 20 (4), pp. 895-913.

Europa (2017), "Employment and social affairs" (in Greek), available at https://europa.eu/european-union/topics/employment-social-affairs_el (accessed on 23/9/17).

European Commission (2016), "The European Union explained-Competition" (in Greek), available at https://publications.europa.eu/el/publication-detail/-/publication/8200c251-aa42-11e6-aab7-01aa75ed71a1 (accessed on 1/11/17).

European Commission (2017), "Priorities-10 Commission priorities for 2015-19", available at https://ec.europa.eu/commission/priorities_en (accessed on 14/11/17).

European Commission/Competition (2015), "European Commission-Competition/Competition-Overview: making markets work better", available at http://ec.europa.eu/competition/general/overview_en.html (accessed on 3/12/17).

European Commission/Competition/ECN (2017), "European Commission-Competition/European Competition Network-Overview", available at http://ec.europa.eu/competition/ecn/index_en.html (accessed on 3/12/17).

European Commission/Competition/ECN/Cooperation (2016), "European Commission-Competition/European Competition

BIBLIOGRAPHY

Network-Cooperation in merger control", available at http://
ec.europa.eu/competition/ecn/mergers.html (accessed on 3/12/17).

European Commission/Competition/ECN/Details (2012), "European
Commission-Competition/European Competition Network-
Overview-More details", available at http://ec.europa.eu/
competition/ecn/more_details.html (accessed on 3/12/17).

European Commission/Jobs (2016), "The EU and Jobs, Growth
and Investment" (in Greek), EU Law and Publications,
October 2016, available at https://publications.europa.
eu/el/publication-detail/-/publication/b9ac1176-9a88-
11e6-9bca-01aa75ed71a1 (accessed on 23/9/17).

European Council/Council of the European Union (2017),
"Competitiveness Council configuration (COMPET)" (in
Greek), available at http://www.consilium.europa.eu/el/
council-eu/configurations/compet/ (accessed on 12/11/17).

European Economic and Social Committee (2017), "Single
Market, Production and Consumption (INT)" (in Greek),
available at http://www.eesc.europa.eu/el/sections-other-
bodies/sections-commission/single-market-production-
and-consumption-int (accessed on 12/11/17).

European Parliament/Committees/ECON (2017), "Economic and
Monetary Affairs-ECON" (in Greek), available at http://www.europarl.
europa.eu/committees/el/econ/home.html (accessed on 12/11/17).

European Parliament/Committees/IMCO (2017), "Internal
Market and Consumer Protection-IMCO" (in Greek),
available at http://www.europarl.europa.eu/committees/
el/imco/home.html (accessed on 12/11/17).

BIBLIOGRAPHY

European Union/Competition (2017), "Competition" (in Greek), available at https://europa.eu/european-union/topics/competition_el (accessed on 1/11/17).

Feld, Lars P. (2005), "The European Constitution Project from the Perspective of Constitutional Political Economy", *Public Choice*, 122 (3/4), pp. 417-448.

Fialová, Kamila and Schneider, Ondřej (2009), "Labor Market Institutions and Their Effect on Labor Market Performance in the New EU Member Countries", *Eastern European Economics*, 47 (3), pp. 57-83.

Fragoulis, Haralabos, Masson, Jean-Raymond and Klenha, Vaclav (2004), "Improving Opportunities for Adult Learning in the Acceding and Candidate Countries of Central and Eastern Europe", *European Journal of Education*, 39 (1), pp. 9-30.

Gobbin, Niko and Van Aarle, Bas (2001), "Fiscal Adjustments and Their Effects during the Transition to the EMU", *Public Choice*, 109 (3/4), pp. 269-299.

Heinrich, Georges and Hildebrand, Vincent (2005), "Returns to Education in the European Union: A Reassessment from Comparative Data", *European Journal of Education*, 40 (1), pp. 13-34.

Jackson, Marvin (1996), "Guest Editor's Introduction", *Eastern European Economics*, 34 (2), pp. 3-10.

Janáčková, Stanislava (1998), "Convergence for European Union Accession: Challenges for Czech Monetary Policy", *Eastern European Economics*, 36 (3), pp. 80-95.

BIBLIOGRAPHY

Jarvis, David, Dunham, Philip and Ilbery, Brian (2002), "Rural Industrialization, 'Quality' and Service: Some Findings from South Warwickshire and North Devon", *Area*, 34 (1), pp. 59-69.

Jenkins, Heledd (2006), "Small Business Champions for Corporate Social Responsibility", *Journal of Business Ethics*, 67 (3), pp. 241-256.

Kazamaki Ottersten, Eugenia (2004), "Lifelong Learning and Challenges Posed to European Labour Markets", *European Journal of Education*, 39 (2), pp. 151-159.

Kinsella, Ray and Kinsella, Maurice (2011), "The rise and rise of long term and youth unemployment in Ireland: the scarring of a generation", *Studies: An Irish Quarterly Review*, 100 (397), pp. 83-102.

Kogan, Irena (2004), "Last Hired, First Fired? The Unemployment Dynamics of Male Immigrants in Germany", *European Sociological Review*, 20 (5), pp. 445-461.

Kogan, Irena (2006), "Labor Markets and Economic Incorporation among Recent Immigrants in Europe", *Social Forces*, 85 (2), pp. 697-721.

Lipsmeyer, Christine S. and Zhu, Ling (2011), "Immigration, Globalization, and Unemployment Benefits in Developed EU States", *American Journal of Political Science*, 55 (3), pp. 647-664.

Lynch-Wood, Gary and Williamson, David (2007), "The Social Licence as a Form of Regulation for Small and Medium Enterprises", *Journal of Law and Society*, 34 (3), pp. 321-341.

Mahler, Vincent A., Taylor, Bruce J. and Wozniak, Jennifer R. (2000), "Economics and Public Support for the

BIBLIOGRAPHY

European Union: An Analysis at the National, Regional and Individual Levels", *Polity*, 32 (3), pp. 429-453.

Major, Iván (2008), "Technical Efficiency, Allocative Efficiency and Profitability in Hungarian Small and Medium-Sized Enterprises: A Model with Frontier Functions", *Europe-Asia Studies*, 60 (8), pp. 1371-1396.

Newell, Andrew and Pastore, Francesco (2006), "Regional Unemployment and Industrial Restructuring in Poland", *Eastern European Economics*, 44 (3), pp. 5-28.

Núñez, Imanol and Livanos, Ilias (2010), "Higher education and unemployment in Europe: an analysis of the academic subject and national effects", *Higher Education*, 59 (4), pp. 475-487.

Ortiz Avram, Daniela and Kühne, Sven (2008), "Implementing Responsible Business Behavior from a Strategic Management Perspective: Developing a Framework for Austrian SMEs", *Journal of Business Ethics*, 82 (2), pp. 463-475.

Öster, Anna and Agell, Jonas (2007), "Crime and Unemployment in Turbulent Times", *Journal of the European Economic Association*, 5 (4), pp. 752-775.

Overman, Henry G., Puga, Diego and Vandenbussche, Hylke (2002), "Unemployment Clusters across Europe's Regions and Countries", Economic Policy, 17 (34), pp. 115-147.

Palazuelos-Martinez, Manuel (2007), "The Structure and Evolution of Trade in Central and Eastern Europe in the 1990s", *Europe-Asia Studies*, 59 (1), pp. 111-135.

BIBLIOGRAPHY

Parker, Rachel (1999), "From National Champions to Small and
Medium Sized Enterprises: Changing Policy Emphasis in France,
Germany and Sweden", *Journal of Public Policy*, 19 (1), pp. 63-89.

Pelagidis, Theodore and Mitsopoulos, Michael (2014), *Greece-From
Exit to Recovery?* (Washington D.C.: Brookings Institution Press).

Perrini, Francesco (2006), "SMEs and CSR Theory:
Evidence and Implications from an Italian Perspective",
Journal of Business Ethics, 67 (3), pp. 305-316.

Petrakos, George C. (1996), "Small Enterprise Development
and Regional Policy: Comparative Analysis and
Implications for Central and East European Countries",
Eastern European Economics, 34 (2), pp. 31-64.

Petrongolo, Barbara and Pissarides, Christopher A. (2008),
"The Ins and Outs of European Unemployment", *The
American Economic Review*, 98 (2), pp. 256-262.

Pollmann-Schult, Matthias and Büchel, Felix (2005), "Unemployment
Benefits, Unemployment Duration and Subsequent Job Quality:
Evidence from West Germany", *Acta Sociologica*, 48 (1), pp. 21-39.

Pratschke, John L. (1981), "Rural and Farm Dwellings in
the European Community", *Irish Journal of Agricultural
Economics and Rural Sociology*, 8 (2), pp. 191-211.

Russo, Angeloantonio and Perrini, Francesco (2010), "Investigating
Stakeholder Theory and Social Capital: CSR in Large Firms
and SMEs", *Journal of Business Ethics*, 91 (2), pp. 207-221.

Russo, Angeloantonio and Tencati, Antonio (2009),
"Formal vs. Informal CSR Strategies: Evidence from
Italian Micro, Small, Medium-Sized, and Large Firms",
Journal of Business Ethics, 85, pp. 339-353.

BIBLIOGRAPHY

Scott, Peter J. and Kelleher, Michael (1996), "Convergence and Fragmentation? Vocational Training within the EU", *European Journal of Education*, 31 (4), pp. 463-481.

Smith, Jennifer C. (2011), "The Ins and Outs of UK Unemployment", *The Economic Journal*, 121 (552), pp. 402-444.

Spence, Laura J. and Schmidpeter, René (2003), "SMEs, Social Capital and the Common Good", Journal of Business Ethics, 45 (1/2), pp. 93-108.

Stanef, Mihaela Roberta (2012), "Measuring Differences in Urban-Rural Development: The Case of Unemployment", *Theoretical and Empirical Researches in Urban Management*, 7 (3), pp. 44-52.

Steen Knudsen, Jette (2013), "The Growth of Private Regulation of Labor Standards in Global Supply Chains: Mission Impossible for Western Small-and Medium-Sized Firms?", *Journal of Business Ethics*, 117 (2), pp. 387-398.

Sternberg, Rolf and Arndt, Olaf (2001), "The Firm or the Region: What Determines the Innovation Behavior of European Firms?", *Economic Geography*, 77 (4), pp. 364-382.

Stewart, Kitty (2005), "Dimensions of Well-Being in EU Regions: Do GDP and Unemployment Tell Us All We Need To Know?", *Social Indicators Research*, 73 (2), pp. 221-246.

Svetličič, Marjan, Jaklič, Andreja and Burger, Anže (2007), "Internationalization of Small and Medium-Size Enterprises from Selected Central European Economies", *Eastern European Economics*, 45 (4), pp. 36-65.

BIBLIOGRAPHY

Sweeney, John (1994), "On Bringing in the Outsiders: What Price Solidarity with the Long-Term Unemployed?", *Studies: An Irish Quarterly Review*, 83 (331), pp. 265-275.

Tatsiramos, Konstantinos (2009), "Unemployment Insurance in Europe: Unemployment Duration and Subsequent Employment Stability", *Journal of the European Economic Association*, 7 (6), pp. 1225-1260.

Uhlaner, Lorraine M., Berent-Braun, Marta M., Jeurissen, Ronald J. M. and de Wit, Gerrit (2012), "Beyond Size: Predicting Engagement in Environmental Management Practices of Dutch SMEs", *Journal of Business Ethics*, 109 (4), pp. 411-429.

Vasileiou, Ioannis (2013a), *European Unification-A Process of Convergence, or Divergence?* (in Greek) (Athens: Historical Quest).

Vasileiou, Ioannis (2013b), "1980-1999, European Union: The Years of Expansion and Enlargement", *From Hitler's New Europe to Merkel's Eurozone* (in Greek), Vol. 1, Historical Archive of Ependytis, pp. 76-95.

Vasileiou, Ioannis (2014a), *European Unification-A Process of Convergence, or Divergence?* (2nd Edition-Special Edition for Universities) (in Greek) (Athens: Historical Quest).

Vasileiou, Ioannis (2014b), *The Present and Future of the Agricultural Policy of the European Union* (in Greek) (Athens: Historical Quest).

Vasileiou, Ioannis (2015), *The Foreign and Security Policy of the European Union-A Critical Approach* (in Greek) (Athens: Historical Quest).

Vasileiou, Ioannis (2017a), *Climate Change: Manageable Problem or Slow Death of the Planet? Role and Actions of the EU until 2050-The impact on Greece* (in Greek) (Athens: Historical Quest).

BIBLIOGRAPHY

Vasileiou, Ioannis (2017b), *Economic Crisis, Employment and Social Affairs in the European Union-Proposals and Actions to Combat Unemployment* (in Greek) (Athens: Historical Quest).

Vasileiou, Ioannis (2017c), *EU Budget-Issues about the Allocation and Redistribution of Resources in the EU* (in Greek) (Athens: Historical Quest).

Vasileiou, Ioannis (2017d), *European Union and Energy-The Route Towards 2050-Thoughts, Ideas and Conclusions* (in Greek) (Athens: Historical Quest).

Vasileiou, Ioannis (2017e), *The European Union Expansion Into Space* (in Greek) (Athens: Historical Quest).

Vintrová, Růžena (2004), "The CEE Countries on the Way into the EU: Adjustment Problems: Institutional Adjustment, Real and Nominal Convergence", *Europe-Asia Studies*, 56 (4), pp. 521-541.

Von Weltzien Heivik, Heidi and Shankar, Deepthi (2011), "How Can SMEs in a Cluster Respond to Global Demands for Corporate Responsibility", *Journal of Business Ethics*, 101 (2), pp. 175-195.

Walsh, Brendan (2000), "Cyclical and Structural Influences on Irish Employment", *Oxford Economic Papers*, 52 (1), pp. 119-145.

Welbers, Gerhard (2011), "The European Social Fund: changing approaches to VET", *European Journal of Education*, 46 (1), pp. 54-69.

Zamfir, Andreea Ileana (2011), "Management of Renewable Energy and Regional Development: European Experiences and Steps Forward", *Theoretical and Empirical Researches in Urban Management*, 6 (3), pp. 35-42.

IOANNIS VASILEIOU

BIOGRAPHY

Ioannis Vasileiou was born in Athens in 1978. In 2001, he was awarded his Ptychio (equivalent to Bachelor's degree) in Political Science and Public Administration from the University of Athens (Greece). In 2003, he was awarded his first Master's degree (International Political Economy) from the University of Warwick (UK). In 2005, he was awarded his second Master's degree (International Economic Management) from the University of Birmingham (UK). In 2011, he was awarded his PhD from the University of Birmingham (UK) with specialization in the economic and political aspects of the European Union's Regional Policy. Since 2011, he has been conducting academic research on issues related to the European Union and international politics and economics.